Introduction

Chapter 1 5
The Rise of AI in Content Creation

Chapter 2 10
The Leverage of Repurposing

Chapter 3 15
Personalization is Key

Chapter 4 19
The Power of Short-Form Video

Chapter 5 23
Authenticity and Transparency

Chapter 6 27
The Rise of Niche Content

Chapter 7 31
The Importance of Data and Analytics

Chapter 8 35
Podcast Guesting and Hosting

Chapter 9 39
Your 2024 Content Marketing Tech Stack

Chapter 10 44
Stay Ahead of the Curve

About Emanuel Rose 54

Introduction

Are you tired of shouting into the digital void, hoping your content will magically rise above the noise? Do you ever wish you had a team of tireless experts whispering brilliant ideas in your ear, effortlessly crafting captivating copy, and deciphering the secrets of what truly resonates with your audience? What if I told you that team already exists? It's not a group of over-caffeinated marketers; it's the power of artificial intelligence (AI). AI is no longer a futuristic concept; it's the here-and-now reality of content marketing. It's transforming the way we create, personalize, and distribute content, offering unparalleled opportunities to connect with audiences, drive engagement, and achieve unprecedented results.

Why This Book is Your Secret Weapon

This isn't your typical content marketing guide filled with generic advice and outdated tactics. Instead, we're diving headfirst into the AI revolution, equipping you with the knowledge and tools you need to thrive in this new digital landscape.

Unleash Your AI-Powered Creative Team: Discover how AI can amplify your creativity, automate tedious tasks, and generate content that captivates.

Leverage the Power of Repurposing: Learn how to squeeze every ounce of value from your content by transforming it into multiple formats, reaching new audiences, and maximizing your ROI.

- **Master the Art of Personalization:** Learn how to craft content that speaks directly to your audience, building deeper connections and driving conversions.

- **Conquer the Short-Form Video Frontier:** Harness the power of TikTok, Reels, and Shorts to create viral content that captures attention in a flash.

- **Embrace Authenticity in the Age of AI:** Learn how to balance AI-powered efficiency with the human touch, ensuring your content remains genuine and relatable.

- **Navigate the Niche Content Boom:** Discover the power of targeting niche audiences and building loyal communities around your brand

- **Unlock the Power of Data:** Use data-driven insights to optimize your content strategy, make informed decisions, and achieve measurable results.

- **Elevate Your Brand with Podcasts:** Learn how to leverage podcasts as a guest and a host to amplify your reach and establish thought leadership.

- **Build Your AI Arsenal:** Explore the latest AI tools and resources that will revolutionize your content creation process.

Your Content Marketing Transformation Starts Now

If you're ready to embrace the future of content marketing, ditch the outdated playbooks, and supercharge your content with AI, then you're in the right place. This book is your roadmap to success in the exciting new world of AI-powered content creation.

1

The Rise of AI in Content Creation:
Your AI-Powered Creative Team

The content marketing landscape is evolving at warp speed, and artificial intelligence (AI) is the rocket fuel propelling this transformation. While AI might sound like something out of a sci-fi movie, it's very much a reality in today's content creation world. If you're not leveraging AI, you're missing out on a powerful ally that can supercharge your productivity, creativity, and overall impact.

How AI is Revolutionizing Content Creation

Think of AI as your new creative team, working tirelessly behind the scenes to help you:

- **Generate Ideas:** AI-powered tools can analyze trends, audience interests, and competitor content to suggest fresh, relevant topics and angles for your content.

- **Write Faster and Smarter:** AI writing assistants can help you draft everything from blog posts and social media captions to emails and ad copy, often in a fraction of the time it would take you to write them manually.

- **Enhance Visuals:** AI-powered design tools can generate eye-catching images, graphics, and videos, even if you don't have any design experience.

- **Optimize for Search Engines:** AI can analyze your content and suggest improvements to help it rank higher in search results.

- **Personalize Content:** AI can help you tailor your content to individual users based on their interests, demographics, and behavior.

- **Analyze Performance:** AI can track your content's performance and provide insights to help you improve your strategy.

Pros and Cons of AI Tools: Separating Hype from Reality

Like any tool, AI has its advantages and limitations. Here's a quick look at both sides of the coin:

Pros:

- **Increased Efficiency:** AI can automate repetitive tasks, freeing up your time for more strategic work.

- **Enhanced Creativity:** AI can spark new ideas and help you explore different creative directions.

- **Improved Personalization:** AI can help you deliver more targeted and relevant content to your audience.

- **Data-Driven Insights:** AI can provide valuable insights into your content's performance.

Cons:

- **Potential for Bias:** AI algorithms can be biased, depending on the data they were trained on. It's essential to be aware of this and take steps to mitigate bias.

- **Over-Reliance on Technology:** Relying too heavily on AI can stifle your own creativity and lead to generic content.

- **Quality Concerns:** Not all AI-generated content is high quality. It's crucial to review and edit AI-generated content carefully.

- **Ethical Considerations:** The use of AI in content creation raises ethical questions, such as the potential for plagiarism and the spread of misinformation.

Essential Tips for Ethical AI Use and Avoiding Pitfalls

To get the most out of AI while avoiding its pitfalls, keep these tips in mind:

- **Choose the Right Tools:** Not all AI tools are created equal. Do your research and select tools that are reputable, reliable, and aligned with your values.

- **Start Small:** Don't try to automate everything at once. Begin by experimenting with a few AI tools to see how they fit into your workflow.

- **Human Oversight is Key:** Always review and edit AI-generated content to ensure it's accurate, engaging, and reflects your brand's voice.

- **Be Transparent:** If you use AI to generate content, let your audience know. Be upfront about how you're using AI and why.

- **Stay Informed:** The AI landscape is constantly evolving. Keep up with the latest trends and best practices to ensure you're using AI responsibly and effectively.

2

The Repurposing Power Play:
From Video to Viral

In the digital age, content is king, but repurposing that content is the kingdom. Repurposing isn't just about squeezing extra value out of your existing content; it's about amplifying your message, reaching new audiences, and maximizing your return on investment (ROI).

The Repurposing Playbook: From Video to Viral

Let's walk through a real-world example of how you can turn a single piece of content into a multi-channel marketing powerhouse:

1. Lights, Camera, Action: Start by creating a high-quality video or podcast episode on a topic relevant to your target audience. Ensure the content is engaging, informative, and aligns with your brand voice.

2. Transcribe and Transform: Once your video or podcast is live, transcribe the audio into a text format. This transcript will serve as the foundation for your repurposed content.

3. Blog Post Bonanza: Edit and refine the transcript into a comprehensive blog post. Add subheadings, images, and relevant links to enhance the reading experience and boost SEO.

strategicemarketing.com

4. Social Media Snippets: Extract key quotes, statistics, or insights from the video and blog post to create engaging social media posts. Use eye-catching visuals and relevant hashtags to amplify your reach.

5. Short and Sweet: Identify captivating moments or soundbites within your video and repurpose them into short-form videos for platforms like TikTok, Instagram Reels, or YouTube Shorts. Add captions, music, or special effects to enhance engagement.

6. Email Marketing Magic: Craft compelling emails that promote your video, blog post, short-form videos, and social media content. Segment your email list to ensure your message reaches the right audience at the right time.

7. PPC Power Boost: Use snippets of your video and blog post to create targeted pay-per-click (PPC) ads. This can drive traffic to your website and generate leads from potential customers.

Why Repurposing Works

- **Expanded Reach:** Repurposing content allows you to reach different audiences on various platforms, increasing your brand visibility and exposure.

- **Increased Engagement:** By presenting your content in different formats, you cater to different learning styles and preferences, boosting overall engagement.

- **Enhanced SEO:** Repurposed content can improve your search engine rankings, driving more organic traffic to your website.

- **Time and Cost Savings:** Repurposing saves you the time and resources required to create entirely new content from scratch.

- **Maximized ROI:** By getting more mileage out of your content, you maximize the return on your investment in content creation.

Repurposing Pro Tips

- **Quality is Key:** Ensure your original content is high-quality and valuable to your audience.

- **Tailor to the Platform:** Adapt your repurposed content to suit the specific format and audience of each platform.

- **Track and Analyze:** Monitor the performance of your repurposed content to identify what works best and refine your strategy.

Repurposing is not just a trend; it's a strategic imperative for content marketers. By embracing this powerful technique, you can amplify your message, expand your reach, and achieve your marketing goals more efficiently.

strategicemarketing.com

3
Personalization is Key:
Crafting Content that Speaks to Your Audience

In today's crowded digital landscape, generic content is the equivalent of shouting into a void. With endless information bombarding your audience from all directions, it's crucial to cut through the noise and deliver content that resonates on a personal level. This is where personalization comes in.

Why Generic Content Falls Flat in the Age of Algorithms

The days of one-size-fits-all marketing are long gone. Modern consumers expect brands to understand their unique needs, preferences, and interests. Algorithms on social media platforms and search engines are designed to prioritize relevant content, meaning personalized content is more likely to reach the right people at the right time.

Generic content, on the other hand, often gets lost in the shuffle. It fails to capture attention, drive engagement, or inspire action. To truly connect with your audience and achieve your marketing goals, you need to create content that speaks directly to them.

Data-Driven Personalization Strategies for Every Channel

Personalization isn't just about using someone's name in an email. It's about tailoring your entire content strategy to meet the unique needs of your audience segments. Here are some data-driven strategies to get you started:

- **Segment Your Audience:** Divide your audience into smaller groups based on demographics, interests, behavior, or any other relevant factors. This allows you to create content that is more targeted and relevant to each group.

- **Leverage User Data:** Gather data on your audience's preferences, interests, and behaviors. Use this data to inform your content creation and distribution strategies.

- **Dynamic Content:** Use technology to deliver personalized content experiences in real time. This could include personalized website content, product recommendations, or email campaigns.

- **Personalized Recommendations:** Recommend products, services, or content based on individual user preferences and past behavior.

- **Interactive Content:** Create quizzes, polls, surveys, or other interactive content that allows you to gather data on your audience and deliver personalized experiences.

strategicemarketing.com

Brands that are Mastering the Art of Personalization

Let's take a look at some brands that are excelling at personalization:

- **Netflix:** The streaming giant uses sophisticated algorithms to recommend movies and TV shows based on each user's viewing history and preferences.

- **Amazon:** The online retailer personalizes product recommendations, email campaigns, and even website content based on individual user data.

- **Spotify:** The music streaming service creates personalized playlists and recommendations for each user based on their listening habits.

- **Sephora:** The beauty retailer offers personalized product recommendations, beauty tips, and even virtual makeup try-on experiences.

These are just a few examples of how brands are using personalization to connect with their audience, drive engagement, and increase conversions. By following their lead and implementing your own personalization strategies, you can take your content marketing to the next level.

4

The Power of Short-Form Video:
Capturing Attention in a Flash

In a world where attention spans are dwindling, short-form video has emerged as a dominant force in content marketing. Platforms like TikTok, Instagram Reels, and YouTube Shorts have exploded in popularity, offering brands a unique opportunity to connect with audiences in a fast-paced, visually engaging way.

The Meteoric Rise of TikTok, Reels, Shorts, and Why They Matter

Short-form video platforms have seen unprecedented growth in recent years. TikTok, the pioneer of this format, boasts over a billion active users worldwide. Instagram Reels and YouTube Shorts, while newer to the scene, are quickly gaining traction and challenging TikTok's dominance.

So, why should content marketers care about short-form video?

- **Massive Reach:** These platforms have a vast user base, offering brands the potential to reach a massive audience.

- **High Engagement:** Short-form videos are designed to be consumed quickly and easily, leading to higher engagement rates than longer-form content.

- **Algorithm-Driven Discovery:** These platforms' algorithms favor engaging content, meaning your videos have the potential to go viral and reach a wider audience organically.

- **Creative Freedom:** Short-form video allows for a wide range of creative expression, from humor and dance challenges to educational content and product demos.

Crafting Short-Form Videos That Stop the Scroll

With so much content vying for attention, how do you create short-form videos that actually get seen? Here are some tips:

- **Hook Your Audience Immediately:** The first few seconds of your video are crucial. Grab attention with a strong visual, a surprising question, or a catchy sound.

- **Keep it Short and Sweet:** Short-form video is all about brevity. Aim for videos that are 15-60 seconds long.

- **Tell a Story:** Even in a short amount of time, you can tell a compelling story that resonates with your audience.

- **Use Trending Sounds and Effects:** Incorporating popular sounds and effects can increase your video's visibility and appeal.

- **Optimize for Each Platform:** Each platform has its own unique features and audience. Tailor your content accordingly.

How Brands Are Leveraging Short-Form Video for Maximum Impact

Numerous brands have successfully harnessed the power of short-form video. Here are a few examples:

- **Duolingo:** The language learning app uses humor and relatable scenarios to make learning fun and engaging.

- **Chipotle:** The fast-casual restaurant chain creates funny and creative videos that showcase their food and brand personality.

- **NBA:** The basketball league uses short-form video to share highlights, behind-the-scenes footage, and player interviews.

These brands have shown that short-form video can be a powerful tool for building brand awareness, driving engagement, and even generating sales. By embracing this format and creating compelling content, you can unlock a new level of success in your content marketing efforts.

5

Authenticity & Transparency:
The Antidote to AI Overkill

As AI becomes more sophisticated and integrated into content creation, a new challenge arises: maintaining authenticity and transparency. Consumers are increasingly savvy and can often detect when content feels robotic or impersonal. This is why authenticity is more important than ever.

Why Consumers Crave Authenticity in the Face of AI-Generated Content

In a world inundated with AI-generated content, authenticity is a breath of fresh air. Consumers are drawn to brands that feel genuine, relatable, and human. They want to know there are real people behind the content, people who share their values and understand their needs.

Authenticity builds trust. When consumers believe that a brand is being honest and transparent, they are more likely to engage with its content, make purchases, and become loyal customers. On the other hand, inauthenticity can quickly erode trust and damage a brand's reputation.

Balancing AI with the Human Touch: Finding Your Brand's Voice

The key to authenticity in the age of AI is finding the right balance between automation and the human touch. While AI can be a powerful tool for generating ideas and streamlining content creation, it's essential to infuse your content with your brand's unique personality and voice.

Here are some tips for striking the right balance:

- **Know Your Audience:** Understand your target audience's values, interests, and pain points. This will help you create content that resonates with them on a deeper level.

- **Develop a Strong Brand Voice:** Your brand voice should be consistent across all channels and reflect your company's values and personality.

- **Use AI as a Tool, Not a Crutch:** Don't rely solely on AI to create your content. Use it as a tool to enhance your creativity and productivity, but always add your own personal touch.

- **Be Transparent:** If you use AI in your content creation process, be upfront about it. Explain how you're using AI and why it benefits your audience.

Examples of Brands That Are Winning with Authentic Content

Several brands have successfully embraced authenticity in their content marketing:

- **Dove:** The personal care brand's "Real Beauty" campaign celebrates diversity and promotes body positivity.

- **Patagonia:** The outdoor clothing company is known for its environmental activism and commitment to sustainability.

- **Warby Parker:** The eyewear brand uses humor and relatable storytelling to connect with its audience.

These brands have shown that authenticity is not just a buzzword, but a core value that can drive real results. By prioritizing authenticity in your content marketing, you can build trust, foster loyalty, and create a lasting impact on your audience.

6

The Rise of Niche Content:

Finding Your Tribe and Building a Loyal Following

In the vast ocean of content, niche content is like a hidden cove — a place where you can connect with a specific audience on a deeper level. While it might seem counterintuitive to narrow your focus, going niche can actually lead to greater success in the long run.

Why Going Niche is the New Way to Go Big

Niche content offers several distinct advantages:

- **Less Competition:** In a crowded market, it's easier to stand out when you're catering to a specific niche.

- **Higher Engagement:** Niche audiences are passionate about their interests and are more likely to engage with content that speaks directly to them.

- **Increased Loyalty:** When you consistently deliver valuable content that resonates with a niche audience, you build trust and loyalty, leading to repeat engagement and even advocacy.

- **Better Conversion Rates:** Niche audiences are often more likely to convert into customers because they are already interested in your topic and trust your expertise.

- **Stronger Community:** Niche content fosters a sense of community among like-minded individuals, creating a space for meaningful conversations and connections.

Identifying and Targeting Niche Audiences with Precision

Finding your niche is a process of discovery and refinement. Here's how to get started:

1. Start with Your Passions: What are you passionate about? What topics do you have deep knowledge or expertise in? Your passions can often lead you to your niche.

2. Research Your Audience: Who are the people you want to reach? What are their interests, pain points, and aspirations?

3. Look for Gaps in the Market: What topics or perspectives are underserved in your industry or area of interest?

4. Analyze Your Competitors: What are your competitors doing well? What areas are they neglecting? This can help you identify opportunities for differentiation.

5. Test and Iterate: Experiment with different types of content and topics to see what resonates with your audience. Use analytics to track your performance and refine your approach.

Brand Success Stories from the World of Niche Content

Many brands have found remarkable success by focusing on niche audiences:

- **Glossier:** The beauty brand started by targeting millennial women interested in natural, "no-makeup" makeup.

- **The Athletic:** The sports subscription service caters to avid sports fans who crave in-depth analysis and reporting.

- **Peloton:** The fitness company has built a loyal following among indoor cycling enthusiasts.

These brands demonstrate that niche content can be a powerful way to build a passionate community and drive business growth. By finding your niche and creating content that truly resonates with your audience, you can achieve similar success.

7

The Importance of Data and Analytics:
Let Your Content Work Smarter

In the world of content marketing, intuition and creativity are essential, but they're not enough on their own. To truly understand what's working and what's not, you need to rely on data and analytics. Data is the compass that guides your content strategy, providing valuable insights into your audience, their preferences, and the effectiveness of your efforts.

How Data Informs Every Aspect of Successful Content Marketing

Data plays a pivotal role in every stage of the content marketing process:

- **Planning:** Data helps you identify your target audience, understand their interests and needs, and develop a content calendar that aligns with your goals.

- **Creation:** Data can inform your content choices, helping you determine which topics, formats, and channels are most likely to resonate with your audience.

- **Distribution:** Data can reveal the best times and channels for distributing your content to maximize reach and engagement.

- **Promotion:** Data can help you track the performance of your promotional efforts and identify areas for improvement.

- **Measurement:** Data provides the metrics you need to assess the effectiveness of your content marketing strategy and make informed decisions about future efforts.

Key Metrics to Track for Content Performance

To get a comprehensive picture of your content's performance, you need to track a variety of metrics. Here are some of the most important:

- **Traffic:** How many people are visiting your website or blog? Where are they coming from?

- **Engagement:** How much time are people spending on your content? Are they liking, sharing, or commenting on it?

- **Conversions:** How many people are taking desired actions after engaging with your content? This could include subscribing to your email list, making a purchase, or filling out a form.

- **Social Shares:** How often is your content being shared on social media? This is a good indicator of how much people value and enjoy your content.

- **Backlinks:** How many other websites are linking to your content? This is a sign of authority and can boost your search engine rankings.

Using Analytics to Make Informed Decisions and Optimize Your Strategy

The data you collect is only valuable if you use it to inform your decision-making. Here's how to use analytics to optimize your content marketing strategy:

- **Identify Trends:** Look for patterns in your data. What types of content are performing best? Which channels are driving the most traffic and engagement?

- **Set Goals:** Establish clear, measurable goals for your content marketing efforts. Use data to track your progress and identify areas where you need to improve.

- **Experiment:** Don't be afraid to try new things. Use data to test different approaches and see what works best for your audience.

- **Iterate:** Continuously refine your content marketing strategy based on the insights you gain from your data.

By harnessing the power of data and analytics, you can transform your content marketing from a guessing game into a well-oiled machine. Data-driven decisions lead to more effective content, better engagement, and ultimately, greater success for your brand.

8

Podcast Guesting & Hosting:
Amplifying Your Reach with Audio

In the ever-expanding world of content marketing, podcasts have carved out a unique and powerful niche. With their conversational format, in-depth discussions, and ability to reach audiences on the go, podcasts offer a wealth of opportunities for brands to connect with their target market on a deeper level.

Why Podcasts Are a Goldmine for Building Brand Awareness and Trust

Podcasts are more than just audio entertainment; they're a platform for thought leadership, storytelling, and relationship building. Here's why they're so valuable for content marketers:

- **Intimate Connection:** Podcasts create a sense of intimacy and connection with listeners. Hosts and guests share their stories, expertise, and personalities in a way that feels authentic and relatable.

- **Targeted Audience:** Podcasts often cater to specific niches, making it easier to reach your ideal audience.

- **Increased Visibility:** Appearing as a guest on relevant podcasts can expose your brand to a new audience and establish you as an authority in your field.

- **Thought Leadership:** Sharing your insights and expertise on podcasts can position you as a thought leader and build trust with potential customers.

- **Long-Form Content:** Podcasts allow for in-depth discussions that aren't possible in shorter formats like blog posts or social media posts.

Tips for Becoming a Sought-After Podcast Guest

If you're looking to leverage podcast guesting for your brand, here are some tips for getting started:

1. Identify Relevant Podcasts: Research podcasts that align with your industry, target audience, and expertise.

2. Craft a Compelling Pitch: Reach out to podcast hosts with a personalized pitch that highlights your value as a guest.

3. Be Prepared: Research the podcast and its audience, and come prepared with talking points and stories that will resonate with listeners.

4. Promote Your Appearance: Once you've been booked, actively promote your podcast appearance on your own channels to maximize reach.

5. Follow Up: After the episode airs, thank the host and share the episode with your network.

strategicemarketing.com

How to Launch and Grow Your Own Successful Podcast

If you're ready to take the plunge and start your own podcast, here are some key steps:

1. Define Your Niche and Audience: What topics will you cover? Who are you trying to reach?

2. Develop a Content Strategy: Plan out your episode topics, formats, and guests.

3. Invest in Quality Equipment: Good audio quality is essential for a successful podcast.

4. Create Engaging Content: Focus on providing value to your listeners with informative, entertaining, and inspiring content.

5. Promote Your Podcast: Share your podcast on your website, social media, and other relevant channels.

6. Engage with Your Audience: Respond to comments and questions, and build a community around your podcast.

Podcasts are a powerful tool for content marketers who want to connect with their audience on a deeper level, build brand awareness and trust, and establish themselves as thought leaders in their field. Whether you're guesting on other podcasts or launching your own, embracing the power of audio can elevate your content marketing to new heights.

9

Your 2024 Content Marketing Tech Stack:
AI Tools to Power Your Strategy

The right tools can be the difference between a content marketing strategy that sputters and one that soars. In 2024, AI isn't just a buzzword; it's the driving force behind some of the most innovative and effective content marketing solutions. Let's explore four AI-powered tools that can transform your workflow and supercharge your results.

Otter.ai

1. Otter.ai: Your AI-Powered Meeting Assistant

Remember when we discussed the power of AI in content creation? Well, it doesn't stop at writing and design. Otter.ai extends AI's reach into your meetings, transforming them from mere discussions into valuable content resources.

- **Turning Meetings into Content:** Otter records, transcribes, and summarizes your meetings in real-time. This means you can easily extract key insights, quotes, and action items to repurpose into blog posts, social media updates, or even podcast episodes.

- **Research Made Easy:** Conducting interviews or brainstorming sessions? Otter captures every word, allowing you to quickly review and analyze the information later.

- **Collaboration Booster:** With Otter, everyone has access to the same clear record of the meeting, eliminating misunderstandings and ensuring everyone is on the same page.

Learn More

aivia.ai

2. Aivia: Your All-in-One AI Platform

Aivia is like having a whole team of AI specialists at your fingertips. This versatile platform gives you access to multiple AI assistants like ChatGPT-4 and Claude 3, allowing you to automate tasks, build custom AI solutions, and tap into pre-trained AI models for various functions.

- **Content Ideation Powerhouse:** Stuck in a creative rut? Aivia can help you brainstorm fresh topics, catchy headlines, and engaging social media captions.

- **Your AI Writing Partner:** From drafting blog posts and marketing copy to crafting video scripts, Aivia can significantly accelerate your content creation process.

- **Data Analysis Ace:** Need to make sense of customer feedback or market research data? Aivia can quickly extract key insights and patterns.

Learn More

strategicemarketing.com

ⓟ Opus Clip

3. Opus Clip: Extract Engaging Moments (Enhancing Chapter 3)

We've already explored the power of short-form video in Chapter 3. Now, let's introduce Opus Clip, the AI tool that takes your short-form video strategy to the next level.

- **Social Media Goldmine:** Opus Clip extracts short, attention-grabbing clips from your longer videos or podcasts, making it easy to create shareable content that stops the scroll.

- **Repurposing Pro:** Extend the lifespan of your long-form content by creating multiple short clips that can be used across different platforms and channels.

- **Accessibility Champion:** Opus Clip automatically generates captions and subtitles, ensuring your videos are accessible to a wider audience.

[Learn More]

⫴⫴⫴ PodMatch

4. Podmatch: Your Podcast Matchmaker

In Chapter 7, we delved into the world of podcasting. Podmatch is the AI-powered tool that can help you make the most of this powerful medium.

- **Guest Booking Made Easy:** Whether you're a host looking for engaging guests or an expert eager to share your insights, Podmatch uses machine learning to connect you with the perfect match.

- **Grow Your Audience:** Appearing on relevant podcasts can introduce your brand to new listeners and expand your reach.

- **Networking Powerhouse:** Podmatch helps you connect with other podcasters and industry professionals, fostering valuable relationships and collaborations.

[Learn More]

Your AI-Powered Future

The AI revolution is here, and it's transforming the way we create and consume content. By embracing the right tools, you can harness the power of AI to streamline your workflows, enhance your creativity, and achieve greater success in your content marketing efforts.

10

Stay Ahead of the Curve:
Your Essential AI Marketing SaaS Directories and Resources

The world of AI is in constant flux, with new tools, platforms, and strategies emerging at a breakneck pace. To stay ahead of the curve and ensure your content marketing strategy remains cutting-edge, you need access to the right resources. This chapter is your guide to the essential directories, platforms, and thought leadership that will keep you informed, inspired, and equipped to harness the full potential of AI.

AI TOOL REPORT

1. AI Tool Report: Your Comprehensive AI Tool Guide

Think of AI Tool Report as your compass in the vast landscape of AI solutions. This comprehensive directory offers in-depth reviews, ratings, and comparisons of a wide array of AI tools, helping you navigate your options and choose the perfect tools for your specific needs and budget.

Learn More

strategicemarketing.com

℞ The**Rundown.**

2. The Rundown AI: Your AI News Curated

Staying informed is crucial in the rapidly evolving world of AI. The Rundown AI is your weekly dose of AI news, delivering a curated selection of the most important developments, new tool releases, research breakthroughs, and expert opinions right to your inbox.

Learn More

TLDR

3. TLDR: Your Time-Saving Summary Tool

We all know the feeling of information overload. TLDR is your AI-powered solution, summarizing lengthy articles, reports, and documents in a flash. This tool extracts key insights, saving you valuable time and enabling you to focus on what matters most.

Learn More

4. Marketing Artificial Intelligence Institute (MAII): Your AI Marketing Education Hub

Whether you're an AI novice or a seasoned pro, MAII is your source for comprehensive AI marketing education. They offer online courses, certifications, and events that cover everything from the fundamentals of AI to advanced strategies and best practices.

Learn More

5. GPTE: Your AI-Powered Text Generation Platform

Streamline your content creation process with GPTE. This platform allows you to create and share AI-powered text generation templates, automating repetitive tasks like writing product descriptions, social media posts, and email campaigns.

Learn More

strategicemarketing.com

OPENTOOLS

6. OpenTools: Your Open-Source AI Toolkit

For the technically inclined, OpenTools offers a treasure trove of open-source AI tools and libraries. This is where you can experiment, customize, and even build your own AI applications.

[Learn More]

BEN'S BITES

7. Ben's Bites: Your Curated AI Newsletter

Ben's Bites is another excellent resource for staying informed. This newsletter curates valuable insights and resources on AI, helping you discover new tools, learn from experts, and stay inspired.

[Learn More]

8. Authentic Marketing in the Age of AI by Emanuel Rose

My book, **Authentic Marketing in the Age of AI**, delves deeper into this critical topic, offering practical guidance on how to use AI responsibly while maintaining your brand's unique voice and building genuine connections with your audience.

[Learn More](#)

strategicemarketing.com

Empowering Your AI Journey

By actively engaging with these resources, you'll ensure that your content marketing strategy remains at the forefront of innovation. Stay curious, stay informed, and never stop exploring the endless possibilities that AI offers. Your audience will thank you with their engagement, loyalty, and ultimately, their business.

Your Content Marketing, Reimagined

The digital landscape is evolving at a rapid pace, and AI is the catalyst for this transformation. As we've explored throughout this book, AI isn't just a tool; it's a partner, a collaborator, and a force multiplier for your content marketing efforts.

Your AI-Powered Content Checklist

Let's recap the key takeaways from our journey into the world of AI-powered content marketing:

- **Embrace AI as Your Creative Ally:** From idea generation to content creation, AI tools can enhance your productivity, creativity, and overall impact.

- **Leverage the Power of Repurposing:** Maximize the value of your content by transforming it into multiple formats, reaching new audiences, and extending its lifespan.

- **Prioritize Personalization:** Craft content that speaks directly to your audience's unique needs and interests, fostering deeper connections and driving conversions.

- **Harness the Power of Short-Form Video:** Create engaging short-form videos that capture attention, increase engagement, and expand your reach.

- **Champion Authenticity:** Balance AI-powered efficiency with the human touch, ensuring your content remains genuine, relatable, and trustworthy.

strategicemarketing.com

- **Find Your Niche:** Focus on niche audiences to build loyal communities and achieve greater success with less competition.

- **Let Data Be Your Guide:** Use data-driven insights to optimize your content strategy, make informed decisions, and measure your success.

- **Amplify Your Reach with Podcasts:** Leverage podcasting as both a guest and a host to build brand awareness, establish thought leadership, and connect with your audience.

- **Stay Ahead of the Curve:** Continuously explore new AI tools, resources, and trends to ensure your content marketing strategy remains at the forefront of innovation.

Transform Your Content, Transform Your Results

The time to embrace AI in your content marketing is now. Don't get left behind in the digital dust. Start experimenting with AI tools, exploring new strategies, and pushing the boundaries of what's possible. The future of content marketing is here, and it's powered by AI.

I hope this book has been a valuable resource on your content marketing journey. If you're ready to dive even deeper into the world of AI and marketing, I invite you to listen to the **Marketing in the Age of AI Podcast** where we explore these topics in greater detail. To continue your learning and explore additional resources, I invite you to visit **emanuelrose.com**. Here, you'll find even more resources, blog posts, and tools to help you maximize your AI-powered content marketing success.

Thank you for joining me on this exploration of the exciting new world of AI-powered content marketing. I'm confident that with the knowledge and tools you've gained, you're well-equipped to create content that captivates, converts, and leaves a lasting impact.

About the Author

Emanuel Rose was born and raised on the West Coast of the United States. He has spent over three decades earning a reputation in cutting-edge marketing. A renowned expert in the field, Emanuel specializes in branding, advertising, and day-to-day operations at his digital agency, Strategic eMarketing. His passion lies in helping companies achieve business success from the bottom to the top.

Emanuel's unique approach to marketing strategies has resulted in countless clients reaching their goals.

Emanuel enjoys learning his craft and implementing new techniques and theories for his clients, not only in his home state of Oregon, but around the world. Together with his hand-selected staff, Emanuel creates opportunities while solving challenges in the ever-changing digital landscape. He is a firm believer in using his personal experiences to help others and this dedication continues to impress.

Not to be outdone on the digital battlefields, Emanuel is an avid outdoorsman. He feels connected to the planet wandering the towering forests or absorbing the energy pouring in from the ocean. His childhood fantasy of discovering those special wild places translates to his writings. The freedom and joy in exploring the natural world is a welcome addition to his life.

strategicemarketing.com

More Marketing Books by Emanuel Rose

Emanuel Rose, a seasoned marketing expert, offers a diverse collection of books designed to equip marketers with the knowledge and strategies needed to thrive in the ever-evolving landscape of modern marketing.

Authentic Marketing in the Age of AI

Authentic Marketing in the Age of AI is a guide for marketers looking to create effective marketing strategies in the era of AI. It covers topics such as understanding authentic marketing, the impact of AI on marketing, building authentic marketing strategies, engaging customers authentically, measuring the effectiveness of marketing efforts, overcoming challenges, and leveraging AI tools. It provides practical insights and strategies for marketers to stay ahead of the curve and achieve marketing success in the age of AI.

Authenticity: Marketing to Generation Z

Emanuel dives into the demographics of Generation Z and explores successful marketing campaigns that hit the bullseye with this generation. He guides readers through the process of developing a fully-fledged marketing plan and web presence that will make them a pro at reaching both Business to Business (B2B) and Business Consumer (B2C) campaigns.

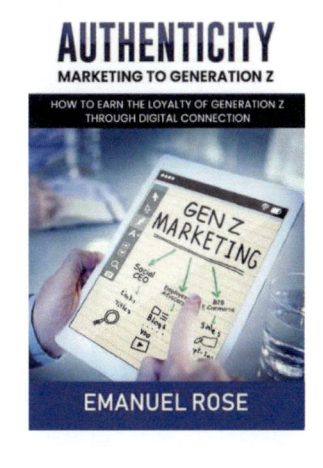

strategicemarketing.com

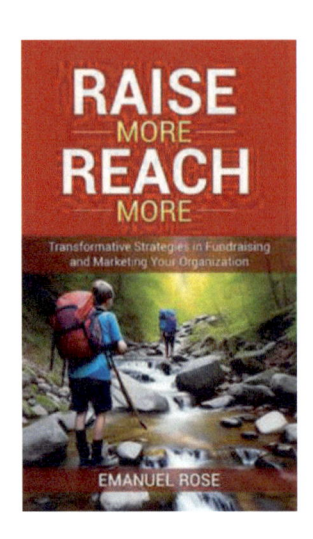

Raise More, Reach More

Raise More, Reach More is a guide to unleash the power of innovative fundraising and lead your non-profit to success with Raise More, Reach More. This ground-breaking guide is tailored explicitly for executive directors, marketing professionals, and all those involved in nature restoration, adventure programming, and child-centered nature initiatives.

The Social Media Edge

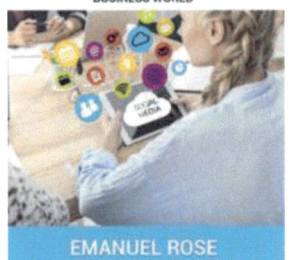

The Social Media Edge is a guide for executives to leverage the social CEO, employee advocacy, and social media to boost their brand image. The book covers topics such as understanding the role of employee advocacy, the social CEO phenomenon, building a social media advocacy program for employees, creating content, best practices, measuring success, and success stories. It also provides insights on developing effective content strategies, using paid social ads, and internal communications, creating a social media policy, analyzing, and optimizing performance, and using video to enhance employee advocacy.

Made in the USA
Columbia, SC
27 September 2024